CONTENTS

WORD HUNT

Look for these words as you read. They will be in **bold**.

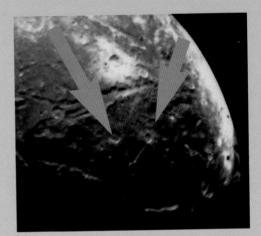

craters
(**kray**-turz)

solar system
(**soh**-lur **siss**-tuhm)

Titania
(tuh-**tane**-yuh)

Miranda
(muh-**ran**-duh)

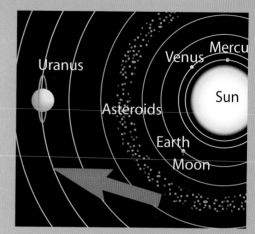

orbit
(**or**-bit)

Uranus
(**yur**-uh-nus)

Voyager 2
(**voi**-ij-uhr 2)

5

Uranus!

Uranus has clouds of gas. The gas is very cold.

Closer to the planet the gas turns into icy slush.

7

Uranus is the seventh planet from the Sun.

Uranus is one of the biggest planets in our **solar system**.

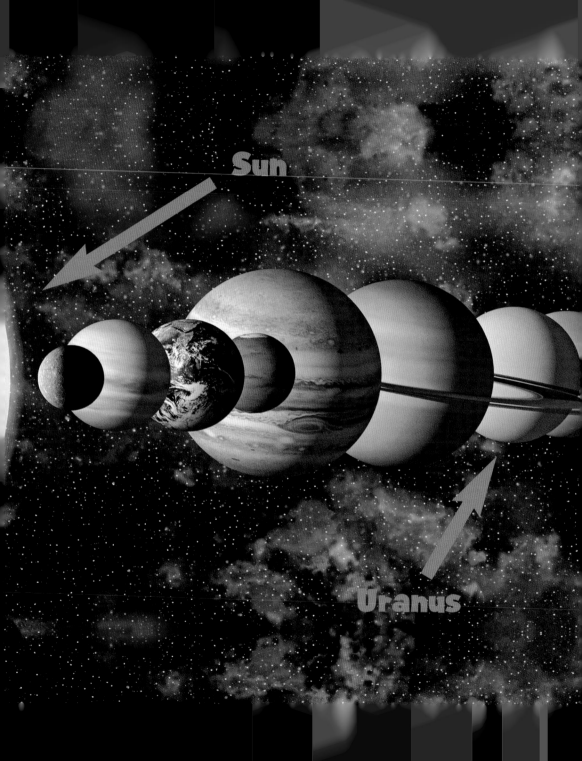

Sun

Uranus

Uranus travels around the Sun on a path called an **orbit**.

Most planets also spin like tops along their orbits. But Uranus spins like a ball rolling.

Scientists think Uranus was hit by something that tipped it sideways.

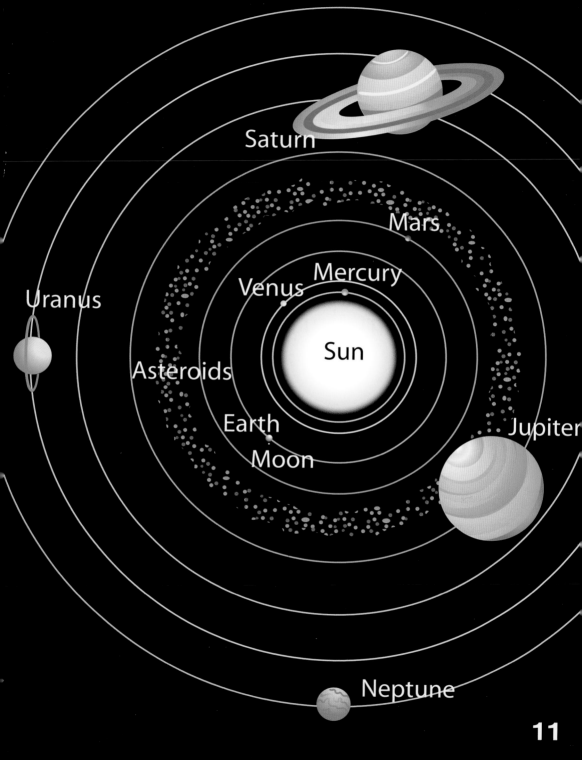

Uranus has 11 rings.

They are hard to see.

The rings on Uranus are made of ice. The ice is covered in dark dust.

13

Uranus has at least 27 moons.

The largest moon is **Titania**.

Titania has **craters**, like Earth's moon.

It also has long, deep marks that stretch around it.

crater

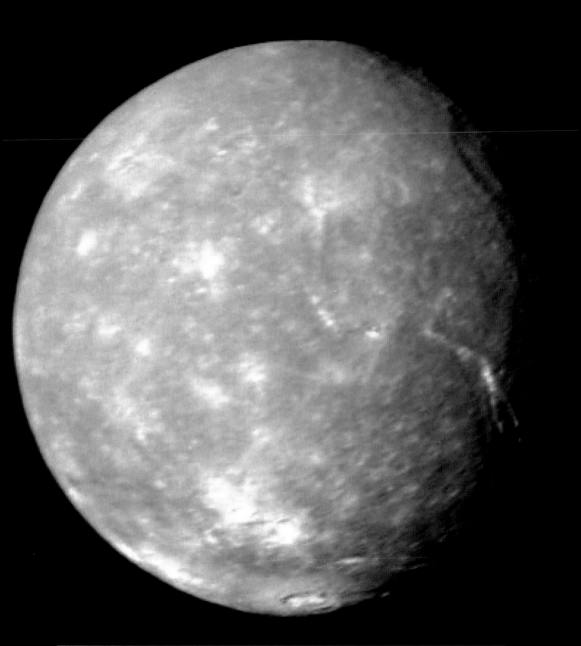

Titania was first seen in 1787.

Miranda is also one of Uranus's moons.

Miranda is one of the oddest worlds anywhere.

It has craters. It has long marks. It has broken rocks. It has giant cliffs.

Scientists know how Miranda got some marks, but they do not know about them all.

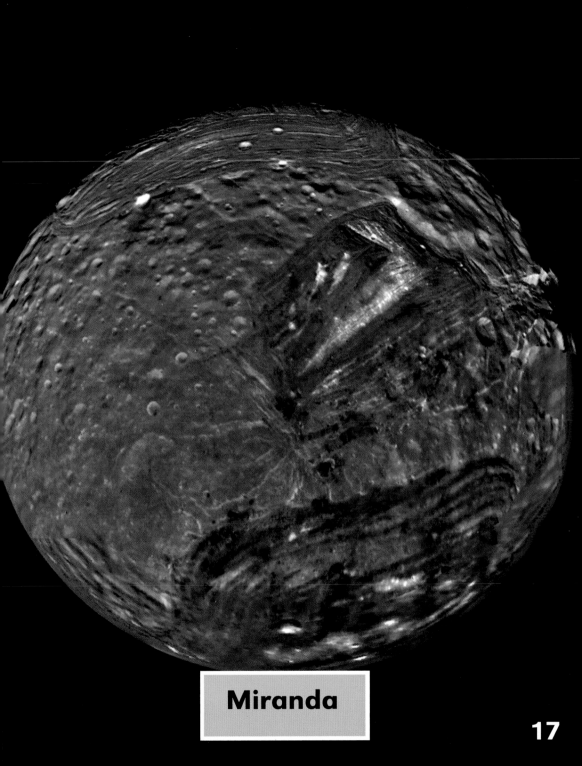

Miranda

Voyager 2 is a space probe.

It is the only craft to go near Uranus.

It is why we know more about this planet.

Thank you, *Voyager 2*!

Voyager 2 first went into space in 1977.

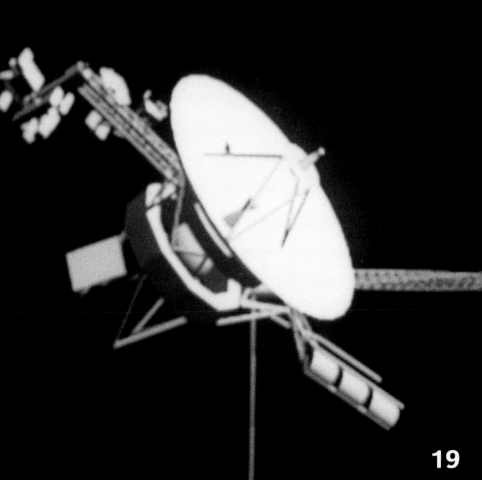

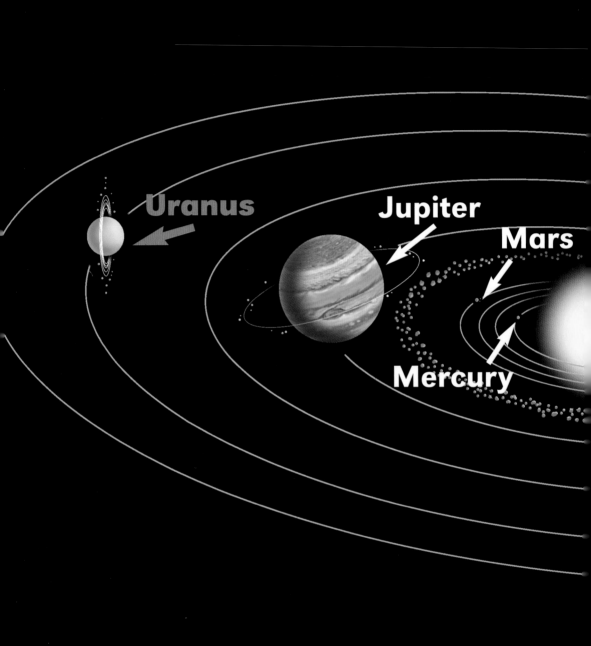

Uranus

Jupiter

Mars

Mercury

URANUS

IN OUR SOLAR SYSTEM

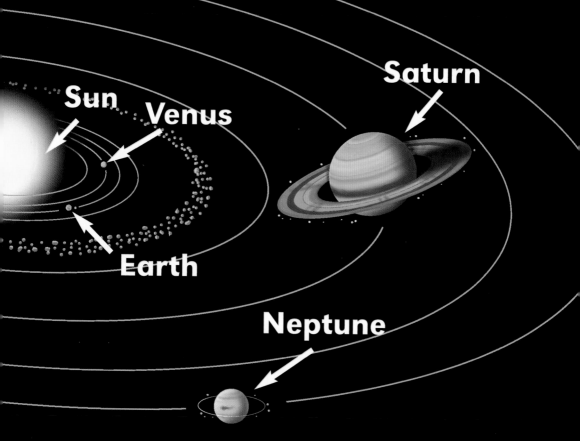

Sun

Venus

Earth

Saturn

Neptune

YOUR NEW WORDS

craters (**kray**-turz) large dents or holes in an object

Miranda (muh-**ran**-duh) one of Uranus's moons

orbit (**or**-bit) the path an object takes around another object

solar system (**soh**-lur **siss**-tuhm) the group of planets, moons, and other things that travel around the Sun

Titania (tuh-**tane**-yuh) Uranus's largest moon

Uranus (**yur**-uh-nus) a planet named after the Greek god of the sky

Voyager 2 (**voi**-ij-uhr 2) the first and only space probe to visit Uranus and Neptune

Earth and Uranus

A year is how long it takes a planet to go around the Sun.

 1 Earth year =365 days

1 Uranus year =30,687 Earth days

A day is how long it takes a planet turn one time.

 1 Earth day = 24 hours

1 Uranus day = 17 Earth hours

A moon is an object that circles around a planet.

 Earth has 1 moon.

Uranus has at least 27 moons with more being found all the time.

Scientists do not agree on which way is North on Uranus.

INDEX

FIND OUT MORE

Book:
Burnham, Robert. *Children's Atlas of the Universe.* Pleasantville, NY: Reader's Digest Children's Publishing, Inc., 2000.

Web site:
Solar System Exploration
http://sse.jpl.nasa.gov/planets

MEET THE AUTHOR

Christine Taylor-Butler is the author of more than twenty books for children. She holds a degree in Engineering from M.I.T. She lives in Kansas City with her family, where they have a telescope for searching the skies.